ALWAYS
A WOMAN

ALWAYS
A WOMAN

by Kaylan Pickford

photography by

J. Frederick Smith

BANTAM BOOKS

TORONTO · NEW YORK · LONDON · SYDNEY

ALWAYS A WOMAN

A Bantam Book/December 1982

All rights reserved.
Copyright © 1982 by Kaylan Pickford and J. Frederick Smith.
Cover photo copyright © 1982 by J. Frederick Smith.
Photographs printed by Sean Smith.

Book designed by Renée Gelman.

ISBN 0-553-01428-5

Published simultaneously in the United States and Canada

Bantam Books are published by Bantam Books, Inc. Its trademark,
consisting of the words "Bantam Books" and the portrayal of a rooster, is
Registered in U.S. Patent and Trademark Office and in other countries.
Marca Registrada. Bantam Books, Inc., 666 Fifth Avenue, New York,
New York 10103.

PRINTED IN THE UNITED STATES OF AMERICA

0 9 8 7 6 5 4 3 2 1

*This book is dedicated to the memory
of my mother, Dorothy White Woodbridge.*

Whatever life asked she answered with love.

FROM THE PHOTOGRAPHER

For the past twenty-five years I have been photographing young and exciting "professional beauties," girls who have become models, the superstars of their world. They are the commodity that sells fashion, beauty, automobiles, food, wine, and all the products we rush out to buy. They are a select few, and in general range in age from sixteen to twenty-five.

A few years ago I was commissioned to do a series of photos for a national hair product, and the client decided to use "women of that certain age"—a charming French expression for women in their middle life.

It was an interesting and enlightening series. I discovered that some of the women I had photographed at nineteen were now forty—even more beautiful and more exciting. The years had given them finesse, sparkle, humor, and a wonderful sexiness.

One woman in particular stood out, and I felt a great urge to understand and photograph this "woman of that certain age." During the next year I devoted my spare time to making pictures of Kaylan Pickford. It was a rewarding and touching experience.

In the past my gray-haired ladies had been cast as mothers, grandmothers, ladies promoting pharmaceuticals and various forms of insurance. Kaylan explained to me that in the advertising world, models in her age-group were sort of second-class citizens. Sexuality was considered appropriate for only the very young, so only those models were given the so-called glamor products to promote. It became apparent that the youth cult was keeping from us another equally exciting world of feminine beauty.

Kaylan, I discovered, had not begun to model until she was forty-five, unlike most professionals, who generally start as teenagers. Her past years had been devoted to a totally different world: two joyful, but tragic, marriages; raising and educating two daughters; rebuilding a shattered life.

Her intense experiences with love and tragedy had helped to evolve a certain style and a sense of humor. She may have lost her girlish laughter, but she became earthy, sensuous. She had acquired humility and had become an exciting woman.

The photographs in this book are a collection of pictures taken over the last five years—a personal diary that reinforces Kaylan's statement that love and sensuality grow with the years and that after thirty a deeper and more telling beauty and sexuality are formed.

These pictures were taken in the early stages of Kaylan's career to give her modeling experience in an area not expected of the mature model, an area at that time lacking. Most of these pictures, however, were taken for the sheer joy of picture making, an artist's delight in the female form.

I have used my camera as the eyes of a lover and discovered that a woman should feel free to express her beauty and energy, to share excitement and laughter, at any age of her life.

J. Frederick Smith

FROM THE AUTHOR

Nothing in my past could have foretold the direction my life has taken. To the contrary: my ultraconservative New England background would never have permitted such an idea to reach fruition.

My early education began in a private school in Boston but changed abruptly to a rural country school when my family moved to eastern Connecticut. We were four grades in one room with an outdoor privy and a water pump. During my teens I spent five insulated and regulated years in an exclusive girls' boarding school. Three years later I left the Boston Museum School of Fine Arts to marry a charming and gifted piano-playing Yale University student.

During our first year of marriage I worked while my husband finished college. We spent a year abroad, then struggled for three years while he finished law school. By then we had become the parents of two daughters. At the end of five more years we were separated and pursuing an agonizing divorce.

My children claimed my life as I did theirs. We slowly made the painful adjustments to being on our own, but there was a deep sadness. We were constantly confronting the wound, opened by a society in which divorce was still unacceptable and where there were few places for a single woman.

The direction of my life changed again two years later when I met Bill, a California man. My eastern reserve and cautiousness dissolved as I began to discover through his love the woman in me. In a year we were married, and life brimmed over with both richness and demands of which I had never dreamed.

Along with my two children, five stepchildren filled a new house and swimming pool with noise, laughter, and tears during the hot Washington, D.C., summers. A stepson, an emotionally upset and dyslexic child, stayed to live with us. In the winters Bill and I took short trips to flee the cold, but the trips served mostly to help us escape the medical demands that had taken over our lives. Bill was dying.

A month following our wedding it was diagnosed that he had cancer. After a four-and-a-half-year fight for his life he died on New Year's Eve, 1968.

In the next year or so my children left home for various schools; I was approaching forty and I was alone. Loneliness and grief enveloped me. I had no vision, no direction. I withdrew.

In time I accepted the truth that my life would not change until I changed it. I recognized that everything I had learned and had come to understand would be meaningless if I failed to use myself. I needed to let go of inner pain, to move into life. I needed to work.

Through the years instinct had made me care about my appearance. Looking well was part of the armor I used to help sustain a sense of well-being during difficult times. Through a vibrant physical appearance, I wanted to project an inner strength that was reassuring to the children and to my husband, and this established a discipline and an attitude that helped me as I learned to live alone.

Without references or guidance, I blindly and naively made my way into the modeling world, into a career and a new life.

This book is the result of my realization, my understanding, and my desire to show that a woman's life is truly lived between youth and old age.

KAYLAN PICKFORD

INTRODUCTION

I do not understand clearly, even today, what compelled me, a widow in my forties, to move to New York City. I understand only a few things concerning that decision: that I was low on energy and was attracted by the high energy level in Manhattan. I knew I wanted "to do something," but I didn't know what. I believe now that I harbored some vague feeling that I might be carried or moved by waves of energy toward something, and, as completely remote as it seemed to me at that time, I wanted to do something that might be helpful to others as well as to myself. I had always been attracted by what is called creative work, but just as I knew I could never stay in a structured nine-to-five job, I also knew I had to begin to earn money.

I had some financial cushioning at the time of my move, but I was paying for my daughters' college educations, one at Harvard, the other at Yale, and though one had a small student loan and the other a partial scholarship, the amount left to be paid was colossal. I knew that those expenses, combined with the cost of living in the city, would not permit me to remain financially protected for very long.

Writing interested me, and a first attempt, a story about my husband's death, had been published in the *New York Daily News Sunday Magazine* shortly after my move to the city. It had attracted a little attention, an offer from a screen writer and an agent. I was sufficiently encouraged to think I might write, but during that first year in New York I found I was not ready to accept the isolation writing demanded. I was distracted by a need to be out among people, to be involved somehow in the flow of life.

I had always been a little shy. My shyness had intensified as I had become increasingly introspective during the years of my husband's illness. I was aware that I was struggling, as I

looked for some sort of identification for myself in my new life. I was fighting aloneness and loneliness. I knew almost no one in the city, and I felt inadequate and unable to pit myself against a society that held scant interest in a middle-aged woman, particularly one without a resume for work. I was frightened.

In time I recognized what was in my way. It was not the problem of what "to do," but the fears I attached to the problems of what "to do." I realized I had to outgrow shyness to be able to present myself for work. If lack of self-confidence was the major obstacle in my way, then I reasoned that it was what needed to be overcome first.

It was a cold, depressing day during my second winter in the city when I reached for my phone to dial a number I had read on an advertisement for a course in learning how to act for commercials. What had attracted me was that it said "small classes." The male voice that answered was kind, easy, and even reassuring as he suggested I come in and meet him. I did, but not because I had any intention or even interest in commercials. I went because I knew I had to do something that would force me to stand up and speak in front of others.

I had no way of knowing that that phone call was the starting point for what would become my career. If the man's voice on the other end of the phone that day had been abrupt or rude I would never have gone to meet him. My insecurity was that great, and my emotions that fragile.

During the course, the class was taught some procedures for trying to get to see tv agents. After some months of procrastination, I went to see a few. In general, I was not very successful or very well qualified, but in one office I was asked if I "did print." I couldn't answer because I didn't know what "doing print" meant. My silence prompted the agent to ask again. This time she said, a little impatiently, "You do model?" I heard myself answer, "Yes."

It was not until I became involved in modeling that I realized how profoundly society is conditioned, molded, and moved by advertising. What came to interest me was not so much where I was used as a model, but where I wasn't used—which was almost everywhere.

There is disquiet in women's souls about not being young, and we live in a society that has fostered that disquiet. I think it is understandable if a woman's sense of herself, of her sexuality, has been threatened because she is no longer young. The myth that only the young are beautiful, desirable, and therefore good for love and sex has been cultivated and perpetuated by business and advertising since the early sixties.

We know that sex is what is used for selling— both explicitly and implicitly—and it seems clear that the leaders of business and advertising either felt or reasoned that for women there is no sexuality after approximately age thirty.

We became conditioned to a country of and for youth. If it was almost all we saw, it was almost all we were offered. Rarely did we see the image of the woman who is variously called "mature," "middle-aged," "older," or even "old." When you did see her she was usually pictured in pharmaceutical ads for menopause drugs, dentures, hemorrhoids, laxatives, arthritis, nearly any bodily problem that involved repairs. The image of her was clear.

If the mature female was not profitable to the money men or to the word men in any positive or sensual way, then who needed her? She was almost never associated with those products that are called "glamorous" in the advertising industry. Apparently she never drove automobiles, drank liquor, smoked cigarettes, used cosmetics, lotions, creams, suntan oils, hair products, perfumes, or wore clothes.

Until very recently tv and films kept the role of wife and mother intact by showing a woman ever patient, ever adoring, ever in the kitchen or laundry, and ever neuter. Anyone physically attractive was too threatening and was not to be reckoned with. If she was beautiful or glamorous she might be a wife (probably a bad one), but certainly she wouldn't be a mother.

The clothing industry barely recognized this woman at all. It catered to youth. Style and elegance became lost in the grab for youthful dollars and encroaching costs. Again the mature woman was ignored.

As a model I know that it is possible for an older woman to wear a great deal of the clothing that is shown and pictured on the young, but to millions of women it is impossible to visualize wearing these clothes, because they have had almost no representation, visual or otherwise. This leaves

them in doubt, inhibited by the overriding fear that they would be out of place or look ridiculous if they wore something that is shown only on the young.

Nearly all products concerned with beauty and glamor have been sold to us by some barely lived-in face and body, endlessly reinforcing the idea that we better not get a wrinkle, show gray hair, or grow old.

In advertising, youth is forever. Pictures, traded on without relief, show the fleeting seconds of a female's unflawed, unlined beauty, as though they could be everlasting, forevermore. "Old" got to be a dirty word in this country, and women were frightened into believing that they had to stay eternally in youth to be acceptable.

Youth can be beautiful, but certainly it is only one look, one kind of beauty.

If a woman accepts what has been the prevalent commercial attitude—that only in youth is there beauty, sexuality, and therefore love—she becomes insecure, as she falls into the trap of making unrealistic comparisons. The myth is cutting, a double-edged sword. On one side it is psychologically upsetting and demoralizing for the woman over thirty; the other side is equally damaging for the young girl who becomes afraid to mature. What has she been given to look forward to?

A few years ago I was told by both men and women in the business that I couldn't be used as a model because I "didn't look like women at my age looked." They claimed that women "out there" in the heartland wouldn't identify with me. They would resent me. I did not believe or accept this, and my experience has been the exact opposite. I asked the decision makers if they believed the top young models were representative of the average young girl in the country. They admit she is not. Her look is what allows her to model. My look is what allows me to model. Why is there another standard applied to me? Sadly, the answer is that a woman my age is not supposed to have a great look. I don't mean necessarily youthful, but an attitude, happy and alive, the same attitude youth projects. Specifically, I am not expected to convey anything sexual or sensual.

I am angry and appalled by this thinking.

Where does this attitude come from? Why has it persisted in spite of education and freedom in a permissive society and at a time when 50 percent of women work outside their homes and are very much a force in the commercial world?

I once asked Eileen Ford to tell me about middle-aged modeling. She said simply, "It doesn't exist, and if it does it's a losing proposition." It was not what I wanted to hear, but it was honest and accurate.

What about men during this same period of time? I can't help but think and feel that the litany of advertising these past twenty years—youth is beauty, youth is sex—has had a profound effect on men, too. Mature men were not ignored in advertising. They were included. They weren't used as frequently as younger men, but they were highly visible and usually represented in a positive way. How many pictures has the world seen of the older man with the young, beautiful girl?

Do women really not stay in shape as they reach what one president of an advertising agency called "No Age"? Is this truer for women than men? Even the rather fragile early physical changes that speak of time on a woman are often regarded by men as a loss of beauty and sex appeal. But only in women; for men they are something else.

accepted the notion that after
_ine in terms of appearance
_teriously get better.

agreed to this for so long?
_____ so thoroughly conditioned by
the idea that our time, a female's time, is only
in youth, when she "has it all"? So we are told,
and told.

It may be worth considering that men make up
nearly 97 percent of the top levels of business
and advertising. This is better than it used to
be. It used to be 100 percent.

If men accept, as women have, what
advertising has been saying, it is
understandable that a man would want to
reach for youthful assurances, particularly
when you consider that there apparently were
no visible older women in the country, except
for a few celebrities and the walking repair
kits. Those invisible women—to whom did
they turn for assurances and reassurances?

This raises questions in my mind.

Were business and advertising right in not
using older women for anything glamorous?

Were the business and advertising
communities, run predominantly by men,
simply playing out their fantasies?

Is it because there are so many young in
positions of power and decision making, and
they use only people of their own age?

Is youth so much more? If so, more what?

Are *we* not worth being included and appealed
to?

Is our sense of ourselves so little or so negative
that we remain silent and don't question, while
it is established and reinforced that only young
is beautiful, sensual, and desirable?

The answer seems to be "yes." We allowed
ourselves to be put out to far pastures, and
even as we went we kept our pocketbooks
open.

While the young female has shouldered an
awesome and unwholesome burden, being
made to feel that everything she is she is *now*
and only now, what about the millions of
women who were ignored and made to feel
self-conscious to the point of becoming self-
deprecating in their insecurity at having to
wonder if they could be wanted, because they
weren't young?

I learned and came to believe, living through
those years as a married woman, divorced
woman, mother, stepmother, widow, and
career woman, that as a result of this emphasis
there have been profound psychological effects
on the women in this country that for many
may be only temporary but for others may be
permanently scarring.

I have had my share of those feelings and
attitudes, convinced at times there could be no
comfortable place for me in this society. I was
cowed, bent with the babel I heard and with
the unrelenting images of youth that claimed
all life for themselves.

The struggle for one's self is not easy and
demands the development of inner strength
and self-conviction.

It comes with love.

MIND

I was peaceful.

I don't know what day, month, or even year it was when I began to change, when the self-generated static inside me began to fade away. It lifted as a fog would lift, silently. I had stopped a harmful interior dialogue about myself and had accepted that I was not separate from my thoughts. Rather, my thoughts and I were one—the same. Me.

How a woman thinks inwardly and secretly about herself will reflect outwardly and openly.

There is no hiding.

For a long time the thoughts I held about myself were not loving, and the society I lived in seemed to confirm that my negative feelings toward myself—a woman in midlife—were justified.

But negative thoughts cannot nourish, and our hunger for approval and acceptance keeps us constantly restless, as we search for ways to reaffirm and reinforce our starved identities. We crave approval, affirmation of our worth, and we seek it out, sometimes indiscriminately.

How can we find a loving response from life if all we hear is the din of our own discord?

We think we hide our negative thoughts from others, but when we hold a thought long enough and strongly enough we bind it to us—and become bound by it. Inwardly, we tune ourselves to our thoughts and signal those thoughts to others as well as ourselves.

If we learn to know ourselves by what we dislike about ourselves rather than by what we like, our lives remain in shadow. Only when we are able to accept responsibility for our thoughts will our lives begin to change and move toward light. Accepting our thoughts—our*selves*—is the beginning of love.

Our thoughts create our attitude
our attitude becomes our behavior
our behavior is how we treat others
how we treat others
*   is what we think of ourselves.*

I know shadows. My own. I even found a small measure of misplaced confidence in being right about being wrong about myself. I hugged negatives to me like old friends. I was afraid to lose them. If I lost them I might become—what? Nothing? Nobody?

I kept them. Dire thoughts and fearful feelings ruled, permitting my defensive attitude to prevail.

I had been deeply wounded by the death of my second husband. My world, which had seemed so large and so bright, suddenly narrowed to a dark corner, in which I stood, shaking. I felt anger and frustration at what I believed to be the injustice of life. Those feelings were joined by thoughts of my own ineptness, or insufficiency, thoughts that I couldn't identify, only feel. I understood dependency; I did not know self-sufficiency, I did not know how to move toward it, or even if I could.

My behavior mirrored my thinking. I felt alone. I saw myself alone. I was alone.

It would have been easier to stay in the corner than to come out, but if I chose to keep my back to life I could only be defensive. What else can you be from a corner?

Life would have left me behind without even a nod, just where I stood, unless I cared enough to step toward it.

Life, after all, would not miss me, it would be I who would miss life.

Our choices in life are made according to our sense of our own worth.

What was I worth? Did I have value? Surely I had learned something, had sacrificed something, had contributed something as a wife, a mother. From the beginning of time society has claimed that woman is important— in the home. Were a husband and children the only measure of a woman's worth?

Advertising has made the mature woman invisible, fashion has ignored her, movies ignore her, business has accepted her only reluctantly, under pressure. We have all been led to understand that a female over thirty is no longer desirable—for almost anything. Especially not for loving.

At thirty-eight I was no longer a wife, and my children were away. Home had become a house. Who was I? Where was the me I knew, or thought I knew? What had happened to the worth I had as a wife and mother? All gone? What value was there to all I had learned, all I had given, to the love I had held? Was I now to be less of a person?

I would be less only if I thought I was less.

Decisions cannot be made until you know what you want. In time I came to know what I wanted. I chose growth. Life is growth. To choose otherwise would dishonor and would negate everything I had become.

I was worth more than any fear I felt in the face of the unknown.

*It is sometimes hard to recognize life's offerings.
They can come in strange disguises.*

How could I understand the future when I
didn't know what it meant, when I didn't
know what I would do, could do?

I felt as though I were sitting alone in a dark
movie theater, looking at the blank screen. At
the top of the screen was written a title: *This Is
Your Future.* I stared at the screen, but was
unable to project myself onto it except in parts
I had already played: Wife, Mother. I was my
own past.

Slowly, I sorted through my feelings. I took
my first hard look at age. I was in midlife, all
alone. I knew that feeling dependent was
emotionally crippling. It caused fear, and when
fear came it never came by itself, but with
relatives: inertia, depression, a sense of
worthlessness. Fear steals your energy while it
holds you hostage.

It took a long time before I asked the obvious
question: What do I want? I had no answer. I
knew that I didn't know. When the response
to my question surfaced consciously, it was
direct: Find out.

I mentally wrote on the blank screen.
    I have my life.
    I will make it good for myself.

The pain of loss, the loneliness, the anger, and
the frustration would have to be converted to
fuel, energy for new growth and new life.
Another me.

The blank screen was opportunity—for
whatever I chose.

I had a challenge to meet. Myself.

If your past dominates your thinking, you will miss the present and lose the future.

I once refused an invitation to meet a man for dinner. I was busy being depressed. Two days later the invitation was offered again. A second chance. I accepted reluctantly. A year later I married the man.

I know how hard it is to love life in the present when you are squeezed by pain from the past. But the truths we learn from experience, like nuggets of gold, shine out. If we seize them they make us richer and more secure in our present, more sensitive to the good we have, less demanding of others, and not so afraid to reach for the future.

If you stay behind too long you will get lost.

The greatest strength is the strength it takes to explore your fears.

When my first marriage failed after ten years, and I was alone with two small children, I was unprepared for what is often thought to be freedom. You cannot know yourself fully, or trust yourself fully, when you agree to have the limits of your life conditioned and set by others.

The trip from dependence to independence needs care and nurturing. You must want to make the trip. No one can take it for you. Like anything intangible, you cannot see your destination. But you will know when you have arrived: you will trust yourself.

More often than not, where there is trust there is love. Your own.

Our lives are often the result of who we are told we are—not who we are.

I began to realize I had labels pasted inside my mind. They had begun to accumulate at my beginning. They said things like Baby, Little Girl, Good Girl, Bad Girl, Adolescent, Teenager, Boy-Crazy Girl, Fiancée, Bride, Wife, Mother, Divorcée, Stepmother, Widow, Model, Actress, Middle-Aged Female.

I thought I was the labels. I am not.

Labels are there for other people to use to identify us. They are not who we are. At the very most, labels define temporary states or fleeting times in our lives. If our only self-identification is by a label, we have lost track of ourselves.

When the structure of the life I had known vanished, no label I had ever had held meaning for me. I felt like there was nobody inside me. I wanted to find myself.

With caring and work, love taught me—me.

I'm free because I've learned to make choices for my own good.

Our country is awash with words and images. As if on a raft, we drift on the currents of marketing. We want to hear something, to see something reassuring, something that will reinforce our lives. We are vulnerable and are easily led away from our real selves. Illusion beckons.

Our freedom to choose means we are responsible for the results of how and what we choose. I have often examined the poor choices I have made in my life and wondered at my failure to be discerning. I go wrong either when I don't listen or when I refuse to take direction from myself. That is, when I don't heed my intuition.

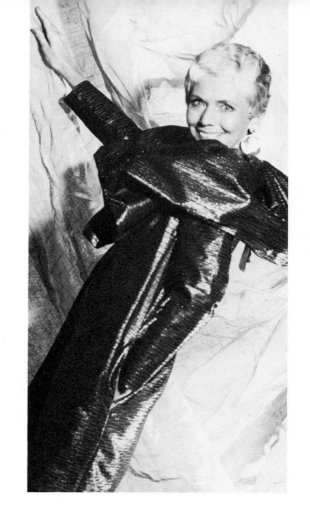

The only failure is the failure to love oneself.

Failure suggests an inability to do something successfully. I could say, the only failure is one's inability to love oneself. Failure also suggests loss. I could say, the only failure is the loss of love for oneself. Whether we are unable to love, or have lost love, or simply fail to love ourselves, the result is the same. When we are out of harmony and lack self-confidence, we often feel dislike for ourselves instead of love.

We have been helped to dislike ourselves by the society we live in.

Advertising seeks the biggest market to sell to, and in the last two decades, because of their numbers, youth has had its greatest power in history, and business and advertising have had their largest market. Together, they have dominated all the many media. The young were everywhere, portrayed as ideal. If you weren't young—you were out.

The gleam from the spotlight on youth was so bright we were blinded by the glare. It was so dazzling we were sold the idea that youth had a value no other age had. The most dazzling thing of all was how one of the greatest natural resources of this country was made to disappear: women over thirty.

For a long time the appearance of youth dominated the country. The country became a giant costume party, as everyone tried to appear more youthful, more carefree. Everything was acceptable except growing older. There was only one imperative: be young.

The imperative should not have to do with age, but should command us to like—better, to love—ourselves.

Advertising works. Do you?

Advertising works because it carefully selects
its messages to penetrate our consciousness
and, by repeating and repeating the messages
both verbally and visually, lodges them in our
subconscious.

But a truth that has been manipulated to sell is
not the same truth as one that serves.

What are the messages we select to repeat and
repeat to ourselves? The messages we hear first
and most often are our own. How do we see
ourselves? The image we see most often is our
own. But whose thinking influences us and
conditions us? Is it our own?

Many of us have been programmed from the beginning of our lives not to think of ourselves, as though thinking of ourselves was an unacceptable vanity, a self-centeredness that was not "nice."

"Do unto others as you would have them do unto you." But how do we treat others if we don't permit ourselves to love ourselves?

We have been given life. Where does limitation come from? Not from God.

You can't hold light or air or love,
yet there is always an abundance.

BODY

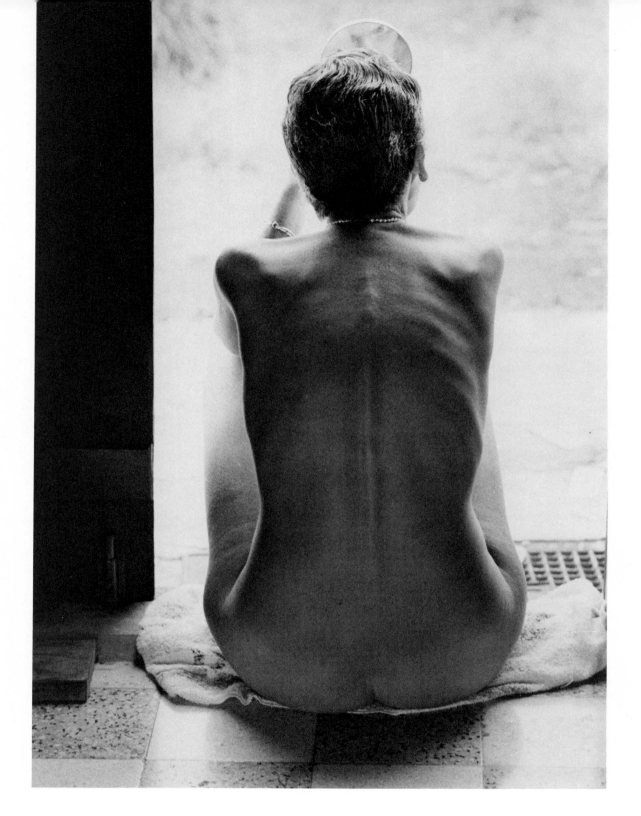

Life is lived between youth and old age

I think of youth and old age as bookends, as
a beginning and an ending that brace, even
embrace, the period of life that lies between
them—the period that is the longest and the
most important.

We take the raw energy and strength of youth
and begin the journey to the other end of life,
to acceptance and maybe even to wisdom. To
make that journey we have to pass through the
middle period. It is in the middle that we try
life the hardest and are tested by it the
hardest. It is where we have our greatest gains
and our greatest losses, where we achieve or
fail to achieve inner growth. It is in the middle
of life that our understanding of who and what
we are must be accomplished.

It is in midlife, as adults, that we learn to
share, not only with partners, children,
associates, and friends, but with the heaves of
life that can either level or raise us. We learn to
accommodate the unexpected with humility in
the face of a force larger than ourselves.

We feel vulnerable when we recognize,
however dimly, that we are moving toward an
ending and that nothing in this world is
permanent, not even us. That revelation
exposes our fragility, a fragility we try to hide
until we can make peace with the knowledge
that we are subject to unseen laws, laws that
we don't make and can't manipulate.

I can remember conversations I listened to as a child, dark, whispered conversations about what happens to a woman in her middle age. None of it was very encouraging. I remember in particular talk about what happens to a woman when her children leave home. Today there is a name for it: the empty-nest syndrome. There were also vague conversations about menopause. The feeling I got was that it was trouble, and it did something to a woman—something that was not good.

Women discuss their emotional problems and
concerns among themselves. Men rarely do.
Although men are less inclined to talk about
themselves, they do think and talk about
women. They also run huge businesses
designed to serve women. Men have been
deciding what women want.

Men get lines. Women get wrinkles.
Men grow gray and distinguished, women
grow gray and old.
Men become heavy. Women get fat.
Men have birthdays. Women don't.

When the gift of conception is withdrawn by
nature, and a woman is no longer able to
conceive, nurture, and deliver life, it does not
mean that she is less or that life is less for her.
To the contrary: more than at any other time in
her life she is free to explore life anew.

I am a woman in midlife. I care more, feel
more, understand more, do more—I am
more—than at any other time in my life.

I am not alone.

Do you compare a flower in bud to a flower open?

A woman, like a flower, goes through many stages in her life. Each stage is different, each is valid. Pretending there is only one stage is a denial of life. Life does not stand still. Only advertising does.

Don't tell me I want to look like some barely lived-in face

I have some lines in my face from fifty years of life. They tell me of years in the sun, of sorrows and joys. They tell me of time. They tell me I have lived and that I am still alive. They can't be erased. They can be softened, but not erased. They are as much a part of me as any part of my body. Do they offend? Would I be better looking, more interesting, without them? Would my life become magically different if they weren't there? If I could have kept my face smooth and unlined, would the events of my life have been different? Would I be different?

Do I long to be the smooth-skinned, freckle-faced kid I once was? No. I long for the same thing today that I longed for then: to be the best I am able to be.

I would feel strange if, looking in the mirror, knowing what I know, I did not see a line from life. Smooth skin goes with the young for every good reason—they have just started.

They have living to do.

If youth believes there is no beauty in age, what does it look forward to? Ugliness?

Once upon a time the words "beauty," "grace," "elegance," "sophistication," and "class" were frequently heard. They were used to describe women, not girls. Older women had mystery. Being older meant knowing something the young could not know, by virtue of having lived. Adults often have a sense of wonder that young adults don't have. They know they don't know everything. That gives them a certain enthusiasm for life that is seldom seen in that stage of life where you know you know everything.

Growing older was acceptable, even normal, when I was maturing. I'm sorry for the young who have been conditioned otherwise, and who have grown afraid to accomplish what nature intended for them.

We bring ourselves to every stage of life. A woman in midlife who loves where she is and knows where she is going understands beauty, grace, elegance, sophistication, and class—and the ingredient that can't be bought or sold—wonder.

I love love stories. I think everyone loves a
love story, most of all their own. Even when
our own love story is intact, we want to see
romance in film or on television. We identify.

I would not want to compare the number of
movie and television stories concerned with
sex and love in young life to the number that
concern sex and love in midlife. If I did so, I
might begin to believe there is sex and love
only in youth.

I don't believe it, in spite of the outrageous
imbalance.

Love and sex in midlife have a greater depth, a finer edge, a more robust understanding, and a more delicate strength, than in youth. The punishments and rewards are greater because we know what youth cannot: time. We understand the lack of it.

Advertising has been very hard on the young.
They have been made to feel that they are
everything. So they have everything to lose.
What's everything?

Their youth?

I was made to feel that I didn't count, because
I wasn't young. So I had nothing to lose.
What's nothing?

My life?

But it is the young who are frightened.
They shouldn't be.

Fear could keep them from becoming
everything they can be—when they are older,
when it counts.

I do not accept the attitude that only in youth is there beauty. Beauty cannot be limited.

I see beauty in young life when it is beautiful. I see beauty in midlife when it is beautiful. I see beauty in old life when it is beautiful.

On the surface what is considered beautiful in youth is the lack of flaws, the smooth perfection. What is considered beautiful in old age is the character of a face with lines and wrinkles. What about beauty in midlife?

Midlife is rarely referred to as beautiful, but midlife women are constantly compared to the young and beautiful females—and found wanting.

It is a mistaken comparison. Since we all grow older we are competing against ourselves. Self-dissatisfaction is not conducive to beauty, and women will remain dissatisfied with themselves if they believe that the only beauty is young beauty. They will lose the race—with themselves.

The look of young life and midlife are different and should be seen and treated differently. Each is special in its own time. When you put the flower in bud next to the flower in bloom you do not try to convince anyone that they look alike.

Some people find the bud more beautiful. They're entitled to their opinion. I like being in bloom. That is what growing is all about. That is what the bud is trying to achieve. The bloom.

While there can be beauty in life that is in the process of becoming, there is also beauty in life that has achieved itself.

That beauty is more than skin deep.

True sex and sensuality come when you know who you are.

My earliest childish forays into sex were explorations of the physical body. I was part of nature. The explorations seemed natural and right to me.

I was lucky. Even when I was taught the accepted coulds and couldn'ts imposed by sexual morality my early instincts and sensitivities prevailed, and I never lost my feeling that sex was part of nature.

Sex can be joyous, or it can be depressing. It can be used as a weapon to punish, or offered as a loving gift. It can be boorish or tender, sad or funny. Whatever its character it demands our attention throughout our lives, and the quality of our sexual involvement is determined by our attitudes.

While our bodies make the sexual act possible, they alone do not give sex meaning: we do, from whatever level of understanding we have attained.

Sex in midlife has the advantages of being young, although not in youth, and of being mature, although not in old age.

While youthful sex can involve bodies alone, mature sex seeks bodies with someone at home inside them.

True sex and sensuality are brought to life from inside of oneself, not from outside. While both seek response, in maturity there is less to prove and more to give.

In maturity we are more.

A woman knows when to say yes and how to say no

It's almost a cliché. Everyone understands that a woman can say one thing and mean another. It happens a great deal. It happens because we are brought up to be good little girls, to be nice, to please, to behave. That means obeying and following someone else's desires. If we disobeyed, or weren't nice or good, we were told we were bad, naughty, and disobedient. Frequently love and affection were withheld,

and we were left feeling we had disappointed, were no longer approved of, and, worse, were unloved. A pattern was formed.

Millions of women are indoctrinated into love this way as children. We learn to bargain—for affection, approval, and love. It is what we are taught. When I was younger I responded this way because I was afraid I wouldn't be loved, and above all I wanted to be loved and thought lovable.

I like to please.

I like to please men.

Women want to please, and oh God how we want to please the men we care about. It's a delicious feeling when we can, but it is only delicious if it is what we really intend to do. When we say "yes" but really feel "no," we are trading: I'll do what you ask, but you have to stay with me, love me.

If we have grown secure about ourselves, we learn that when we say "no" and lose, we haven't lost anything. You can't lose the love of someone who doesn't recognize your rights and your need to be honest. It is not love that is lost, only a cheap imitation.

When a woman knows her worth, she knows how to say "no" and mean "no." She learned it from that time in her life when she felt she had to say "yes"—and meant "no."

When she knows her worth, she also knows when to say "yes"—and mean it.

Not using yourself is like a flower refusing to grow

I know what it's like to not want to get up in the morning and face the day. I know what it's like to not want to go to bed and sleep alone. I know what it's like to not know what to do for days and days.

I remember those feelings. I hated those feelings.

What was I doing that made me feel that way? I was devouring myself with my own energy, with my own life force. I was using it against myself by my negative thinking about myself and my life. When we don't use our God-given energy positively, it will work against us for as long as we allow it to. It can destroy as surely as drugs, or pills, or alcohol, by stopping our growth. Energy cannot stand still. We are energy, and we can't stand still in life. We either progress or regress.

If the flower refused to grow it would die. We are like the flowers. We can't refuse the gift of life. Our work, like the work of the flowers, is to realize ourselves.

Beauty within must be brought to the surface to be seen

The beauty industry suggests that if we get beautiful, that is, young and beautiful, our lives will improve. The fashion industry makes no suggestions: they simply show us everything on the young, and we can take it or leave it. If we take it, the chances are we even have to wear their initials over our hearts or on our sleeves.

How long can anyone be made to feel unacceptable before she begins to believe it and act as though it were true?

Any woman at any age knows that buying beauty is not the same as feeling beautiful, as knowing and believing in her inner beauty.

Even the word "beautiful" suggests more than a facade, more than "pretty" or "lovely." Beautiful is connected to love. I cannot think of anything in life, when it is created with love, that does not contain beauty. I also do not know anyone who is able to love herself who does not grow beautiful.

When I started working as a professional model and met with constant rejection because of my age, they said it was the system. It made me acutely aware of how women in midlife were turned into the ugly stepsisters, while the young Cinderellas danced at the ball. I was tempted many times to give up. Sometimes my feelings were hurt, but mostly it made me angry. I have a value, a worth, and a look, which I did not feel should be diminished because I lived in a society that has been hustling youth and suggesting that I am a lesser female because I am over thirty. I learned not to listen to them. I listened to myself.

We have been told, with a persistence that almost has to be admired, what is wrong with us. Very little is offered about what is right with us. This has been keenly felt by the young, too. They have been led to think there can be nothing either positive or beautiful connected to age.

We should stop listening to the system. They are strangers. They don't know us.

We are not here to hide. We are here to shine.

A woman who casts the light and aura of being beautiful knows who she is

SPIRIT

I am endlessly changing—new, even to myself

Women have made dramatic changes in their
lives during the past decade. Hard changes.
They have questioned the traditional attitudes
that made up the legacy of being female.
Society gave them very little help. Society told
them they were crazy; that they couldn't have
certain jobs; that they were not supposed to do
certain things or be certain ways; that they
were not equal to men; that they should stay
home where they belonged, shut up, not make
disturbances; that they had become hard and
aggressive. But almost no one heard them
when they spoke nicely and politely about the
changes they wanted. Few believed that they
were serious, and it was not until they did
something for themselves, in spite of the
resistance, that they were heard.

In my professional experiences as a model I
have run up against these blocks. I know they
exist in personal relationships, too. When
people hear things that suggest changes in
their lives, their comfort, they resist what they
hear and therefore the person saying it. Only
when we become committed to what we want
to accomplish will change occur. We make it
happen when we take responsibility for our
own lives.

*If someone is comfortable at your expense, and you
don't like it, it is your own fault if you don't change
it.*

When a woman's spirit has been cramped too long it will find ways to stretch no matter what, and trying to stop that movement of life is like trying to dam up the heavens.

We all change. There is nothing alive that is not always changing. Life keeps us in constant physical change from the moment we are conceived until death. Change is demanding, and when we refuse to accept the lessons it offers, we condemn ourselves. Refusal to take responsibility for using ourselves is only another way of avoiding ourselves. And it is a sure way to grow poor in spirit.

If our fear that we are "not enough" is so great that we remain spectators of life, afraid to measure ourselves in the real world, we won't be enough for ourselves, much less for anyone else.

Change in life, if accepted, can be an adventure instead of a threat. It often requires courage. Where are we without it?

We all want self-esteem. It is earned, not given.

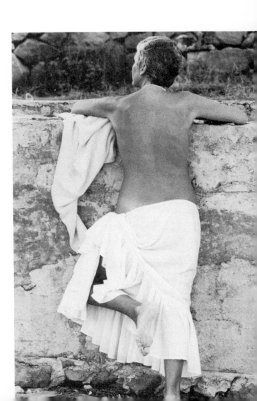

Rigidity of mind stifles the spirit and steals beauty.

As a parent I felt that direction and discipline were helpful and right for my children, but that rigid thinking about how they "should be" was not. They were individual souls who inspired individual consideration and demanded flexibility of thought and spirit from me. I was more careful and concerned about their spirits than I was about my own. While I had always hoped they would feel free and comfortable expressing their desires, they also had to learn that holding a conviction meant acting on it, or it became only a vaporous dream.

I know them. They are beautiful.

When I was widowed I insisted rigidly to myself that I was not trained to do anything, that no one would hire me, that I didn't know anything useful, that I couldn't be beautiful at my age, and that no man would be interested in me. It was a crushing list, but I knew!

No one was keeping score except me, and I was wrong about myself on every count.

I neglected to see myself as individual and unique, the way I saw my daughters. Instead, I fell prey to the business-and-advertising pharmaceutical conception of a woman in midlife. What life? It never occurred to me that Madison Avenue might lack imagination and insight. Without thought I simply accepted their image of the woman in midlife.

Insecurity inspires rigid thinking. We have to know something, be right about something. If we are not right about ourselves—then what?

Rigid thinking about yourself can steal more than your beauty—it can steal your life by stifling your spirit.

Replace every "I can't" with an "I can."

When I look back and recall the things I thought I could not do, all the "I can'ts" I gave myself with utter sincerity, I can see that they were in direct proportion to my own sense of worth at that time. Saying "I can't" was easy.

Learning to say "I can" was not easy, and I sought the help of a psychiatrist I trusted. The process meant evaluating and reconciling the honest and dishonest negative feelings I held about myself. It meant not blindly accepting the ideas about women in midlife that permeated the country—that I had passed my prime and it was too late for me. That in turn meant accepting the startling idea that I could have a full life on my own.

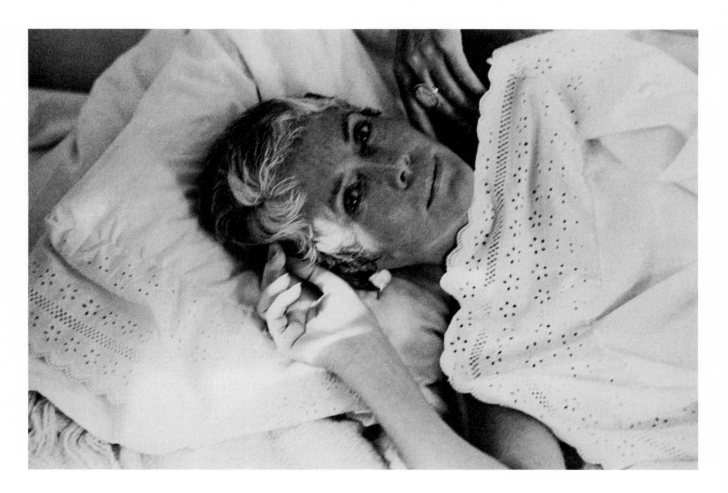

There was no one moment, no great flash of emotional or intellectual illumination, that dissolved pain or released me from my restrictive thoughts. The change evolved gradually. But it evolved only because I worked toward it on my own, as well as with outside help.

I wanted to learn how to prosper, not just survive.
I wanted to know how to truly love myself.
I wanted to understand how to be alone and be whole.
I wanted to be able to connect with life and with other people.

If I had no one close at hand to help or
encourage me, I also had no one to blame. I
was responsible for who I was and how I felt.

I learned to hear myself every time I said "I can't." We are so habitual we are deaf to ourselves. I learned to know something about my anger, my shyness, my loneliness, my sense of ineptness. And I learned not to feel defeated when acknowledging any one or all of them.

I reached beyond what I thought were my limits to become part of life on my own merits, by my own strength, and in my own time.

Everyone has a role in life. No one else can or should tell you what yours is. Though it may be hard work, it needs to be discovered and identified.

Like yourself enough to enjoy being alone.
That is the beginning to the end of loneliness.

Loneliness is a bitch. It invades the spirit,
twists the heart, tears at the ego, and can drive
you to bizarre behavior if you are alone and
lonely too long.

Loneliness forces you in upon yourself, and you can consume yourself worrying about why you are alone. Loneliness can convince you that there is something wrong with you. It doesn't matter whether you live in a shack or a castle, no one wants it. It hurts.

Shortly after moving to New York City I went to a neighborhood bar alone. I felt awkward and self-conscious. I was not going to pick anyone up; I went because I was feeling lonely and wanted to be where other people were, where there was some life going on.

We can surround ourselves with other people, even with strangers or with people we don't necessarily want to be with. We can sit passively in front of a television, refusing to think or feel. We can "just hang around" somebody, somewhere. We can even sell ourselves the idea that we don't need to be loved, that it doesn't matter whether we are cared for or not. And we can bury the pain and anger that exist along with the fear.

Sometimes we believe others should do
something about us or for us, that they should
recognize how we are suffering, and it is easy
to become angry and hurt when they fail to
meet our expectations. But loneliness can drive
expectations out of all reasonable proportion. It
is easy to put others down when we are
uncomfortable with our lives.

One of the worst effects of loneliness is feeling sorry for yourself. I remember.

I remember, too, how energy for living and loving can seep away. We blame "life" or the world for that seepage, but our world is in our minds. We build our world with our thoughts.

There are endless avenues of escape from loneliness. Many are damaging, some deadly. We can choose to confront our fear of loneliness and find the courage to meet it. When we approve of how we are spending our selves—our lives—the pain of loneliness eases.

In time we will find pleasure in our own company, and when we do, so will others.

To make peace with death is to free yourself for living.

Death does not consider age. Death roars its demand that we evaluate what we call reality. It forges new priorities in our lives, bending us like heated metal and forming us again, but differently.

I was thirty-four years old, a bride of a month, two weeks home from my honeymoon, madly in love, standing on the threshold of a new beginning, when it was discovered that my husband had incurable cancer. When he died four years later I had been shaped anew, and forever.

It was inconceivable to me that he whom I loved so much could lose his life. I felt that my world had to include him. I was afraid, unaccepting, losing.

In time I saw I would have to learn to accept what appeared to be irrational and impossible to understand.

Was there a way to find understanding that could be tempered by love? Was there really a higher love that would lead me and show me how to understand?

There was. There is.

When I believed I was seeking understanding, it was really love I was seeking: they are one and the same.

If death could make me bitter and fearful, then I would lose not to death—but to life.

I learned that while death could claim life, it could not claim love.

At no age will I lose my closest friend: the child in me.

I have a loving shadow that lives in me. We are one. I hope, intensely, that it never fades away. It is the child in me.

Children are rich in spirit. They have a natural curiosity; discovery is joyous. Their ceaseless flow of spontaneous ideas keeps them darting, like bees among flowers, from thought to thought, determined to try each one.

Nothing in the imagination is beyond reach. There is nothing that can't be played out or made to happen. Children's understanding of limitation is only that they are too small to do some things or that they don't know how, but will learn if someone will teach them. It is never that it can't be done.

When things go wrong children are unafraid to dream that somehow they will be made right. They have faith.

Joy comes from a well-fed spirit.

Can anyone describe joy? I can't. But I know it is as necessary to the health of the spirit as food is to the body.

Joy leavens. It encourages, even excites the spirit within while it poises our hearts to both give and receive. We gain new vigor for all of life when we are joyful about even one thing in our lives.

It took me a long time to learn that doing what nourished my spirit was not selfish, but essential.

For those who are able to receive it, joy is a message of love. It's infectious.

Laughter strengthens.

Sometimes we forget and have the audacity to think we are running life. Our behavior can be pretty funny, even ridiculous.

If we gain the perspective to laugh at ourselves, we strengthen our egos, and that helps us through those times when we remember who really does run life.

There is beauty in every stage of life if we allow it.

Age does not legislate beauty.
There is no such thing as one standard for
beauty any more than there can be one
standard for how one loves or how one grows,
but in any stage beauty requires attention, no
matter what is happening in our lives.

How we feel affects how we look, and so does
how we care for ourselves—or fail to.

I have always made sure I put myself together at the beginning of each day. I was afraid not to honor myself in that simple and fundamental way. It was the cement on which I built each day. It gave me some sense of control about myself, and if it was the only thing in a day that gave me that feeling, it was very important. It did not matter whether I was putting on blue jeans or a dress, I needed to feel I looked well. I felt, and still do, that if I abandoned that morning ritual it would have been equivalent to saying, "I give up, I don't care."

I did care. Even in moments when I was not sure what I was supposed to be caring about, keeping that discipline helped me connect, in some small but positive way, to inner feelings. Like a keel on a boat it steadied me and at moments may well have kept me from capsizing.

I have spent my life trying to find ways to allow myself to become beautiful, both inside and outside. There is no one day I will achieve it, it is just something to strive for.

In each stage of my life I have resisted and fought anything that threatened my freedom to choose to be as beautiful as I can be. It is every woman's option, as it is every woman's understanding that her sense of her own beauty is an inextricable part of life.

Beauty is not as fragile as our feelings about
ourselves are, but it is elusive, and we have to
keep choosing it and bringing it into our lives.
Our ability to choose strongly for ourselves can
become easily lost when we feel overwhelmed.
While cosmetics can enhance our faces and
bodies to a certain degree, there is no cosmetic
in the world that can make us beautiful when
we relinquish our desire, our freedom, to
choose to be as beautiful as we are able to be.

*Our desire for beauty and our desire for life are
inseparable.*

If life is spirit as much as flesh, hold a loving spirit.

Women in midlife are resourceful, sensitive, and multifaceted. The adjustments they have had to make to the innumerable changes in our society are far more dramatic than those the young have had to face. People in midlife have straddled two worlds: the one they were born into and the one they live in today.

There is no one whose life is not affected by change. Some changes are incredibly difficult, but change itself does not guarantee growth. I believe that unless we are able to uncover love, inherent in almost any life situation, we can't grow in spirit. Our spirits won't be able to strengthen our lives.

Living demands passion, as any creative endeavor does, and passion requires spirit.

It is difficult to prosper in life without encouragement or enthusiasm from others, and there has been little of either proffered to women over thirty in the last twenty or more years.

Women in midlife have had to dig their own wells of understanding, prime their own pumps of appreciation, and drink to themselves for too long.

It has taken strength to stand in the face of the strong prevailing winds that have blown across the country for so long, but encouragement is coming—slowly—because the country is growing older.

Encouragement will come after we have discovered what we already know but may have forgotten—that we have beauty and sophistication and spirits grown strong from living and loving.

There is nothing new under the sun, except the discovery of ourselves. That requires experience. To gain experience we have to try something, do something, feel and care about something. It means we have to reach out and try ourselves on, be willing to expose ourselves.

Experience is the child born of risk.

Any degree of risk has some element of the unknown, but no one courts risk without believing that they have some chance to achieve what they set out to do.

Instinct often dictates the time we choose to risk ourselves. We sense when we are no longer able to ignore some inner prompting, a whisper, that tells us we have to make the effort to begin to learn again, to change our lives, to change ourselves. Sometimes it can mean leaving for strange or distant places for what seem to be strange or foreign reasons. Sometimes we may not even be sure we understand why we are doing what we are doing. We only know that we have to do it.

Any risk, large or small, is intensely personal. It means decision and self-challenge. Only we alone know, in the privacy of our hearts, what personal challenges we've conquered, or failed to, how big was our mountain, and how long was our reach into the unknown.

The results of risk are commonly evaluated in terms of success or failure. But the true and valuable measure of risk is in what we have learned and how we have grown.

We are all responsible for what we contribute to our lives. We have to keep earning ourselves over and over again; if we stop, we truly risk our lives. We risk losing them.

If we choose life and growth, I believe we have chosen love.

I know that in this time in my life I love more than in my youth because I am more.

I risked therefore I have.

When is a woman?

Always.